FASHION IN THE MIDDLE EAST: TRANSFORMATION, INNOVATIONS, AND CHALLENGES

The Middle Eastern fashion industry is a dynamic and rapidly growing sector that has undergone significant transformation in recent years. The industry is rooted in a deep cultural heritage, with a rich history of traditional textiles, crafts, and garments. Today, the industry has evolved to include a wide range of modern and innovative designs, reflecting changing consumer preferences and global trends.

Fashion in the Middle East: Transformation, Innovations and Challenges explores the complex and multifaceted nature of the Middle Eastern fashion industry, providing insights into the ways in which designers, entrepreneurs, artisans, and consumers are shaping the industry and contributing to its growth and development.

Fashion in the Middle East: Transformation, Innovations, and Challenges is a must-read for anyone interested in fashion, culture, and the Middle East. It provides a detailed and nuanced look at the industry, offering expert insights and analysis that will inform and inspire readers.

CHAPTER 1: FASHION IN THE MIDDLE EAST - A HISTORICAL OVERVIEW

The Arab conquests of the 7th and 8th centuries saw the spread of Islam across the Middle East, bringing with it new clothing styles that reflected the religion's modesty requirements. Women began wearing the hijab and abaya, while men wore the thobe, a long robe-like garment. These traditional garments have continued to be worn in many Middle Eastern countries, although they have also evolved over time to incorporate modern designs and materials.

In the early 20th century, the region saw the emergence of a new class of wealthy individuals who began to embrace Western fashion trends. They would often travel to Europe to purchase clothing and accessories, and this trend continued to grow throughout the century. At the same time, traditional garments continued to be worn by the majority of the population.

In the 21st century, the Middle Eastern fashion industry has seen significant growth and transformation, fueled by the rise of social media and e-commerce. Middle Eastern designers and entrepreneurs have gained increasing recognition in the global fashion industry, with many showcasing their work at international fashion weeks and events.

Today, the Middle Eastern fashion industry is a vibrant and dynamic sector that continues to evolve and innovate. It is a reflection of the region's cultural heritage, but also of its modernity and openness to new ideas and influences.

In conclusion, fashion in the Middle East has a rich and complex history that reflects the region's cultural traditions, religious practices, and social norms. From traditional garments to modern couture, the Middle Eastern fashion industry has undergone significant transformation and evolution over the centuries. Today, it is a vibrant and dynamic industry that continues to shape and be shaped by global fashion trends.

CHAPTER 2: CULTURAL SIGNIFICANCE OF MIDDLE EASTERN FASHION

Fashion in the Middle East is deeply ingrained in the region's cultural traditions and identity. Clothing has always played a significant role in expressing individual and collective identities, reflecting social, religious, and cultural values.

In many Middle Eastern countries, clothing is seen as a symbol of modesty and piety, and traditional garments such as the hijab and abaya are worn to comply with religious requirements. These garments have become associated with Islamic culture and are often seen as a representation of the region's cultural identity.

In addition to religious requirements, fashion in the Middle East also reflects social norms and expectations. For example, in some countries, women are expected to dress modestly and cover their bodies, while men are expected to dress conservatively. In other countries, there may be more liberal attitudes towards clothing, with greater emphasis placed on individual expression and creativity.

Fashion in the Middle East is also a means of expressing national and regional identities. Many designers draw inspiration from the region's cultural heritage, incorporating traditional motifs and designs into their work. Fashion weeks and events in the Middle East often showcase the work of local designers, providing a platform for them to express their creativity and showcase their unique perspectives.

In recent years, the Middle Eastern fashion industry has also been at the forefront of promoting inclusivity and diversity. Modest wear, which is popular in many Middle Eastern countries, has become a global trend, appealing to consumers who are looking for clothing that is both fashionable and modest. Many Middle Eastern designers are also exploring gender-neutral designs and promoting greater acceptance of non-binary identities.

In conclusion, fashion in the Middle East is deeply connected to the region's cultural traditions and identity. It reflects religious, social, and cultural values, and is a means of expressing individual and collective identities. The industry is also at the forefront of promoting inclusivity and diversity, challenging traditional gender norms and promoting greater acceptance of non-binary identities.

CHAPTER 3: THE RISE OF MIDDLE EASTERN FASHION ENTREPRENEURS

The Middle Eastern fashion industry has seen a significant rise in entrepreneurship in recent years, with many designers and entrepreneurs establishing their own brands and businesses. This trend is driven by a combination of factors, including increasing consumer demand for local fashion and a desire for greater representation in the global fashion industry.

One of the challenges facing Middle Eastern fashion entrepreneurs is limited access to funding. Many entrepreneurs struggle to secure the necessary financial backing to start and grow their businesses, particularly in countries with underdeveloped financial systems. As a result, many designers and entrepreneurs are turning to alternative funding sources, such as crowdfunding and angel investing.

Another challenge facing Middle Eastern fashion entrepreneurs is the need to balance creative expression with cultural expectations. Many designers face pressure to conform to cultural norms and expectations, particularly around modesty and gender roles. However, this has also led to the emergence of new and innovative fashion trends, such as modest wear, that are gaining popularity both in the Middle East and globally.

Despite these challenges, Middle Eastern fashion entrepreneurs are making significant strides in the industry, with many establishing successful brands and gaining recognition both domestically and internationally. The emergence of fashion weeks and events in the region, such as Dubai Fashion Week and Arab Fashion Week, has also provided a platform for local designers to showcase their work and gain exposure.

The rise of Middle Eastern fashion entrepreneurs is not only a reflection of the region's growing economic and social development, but also of its desire to have a greater voice and representation in the global fashion industry. As the industry continues to grow and evolve, it is likely that we will see more innovative and successful fashion entrepreneurs emerge from the region.

In conclusion, the rise of Middle Eastern fashion entrepreneurs is a positive trend for the region, reflecting its growing economic and social development, and its desire to have a greater voice in the global fashion industry. Despite the challenges facing entrepreneurs in the region, the industry is seeing significant growth and innovation, and there is much potential for continued success and impact.

CHAPTER 4: STATE OF FASHION EDUCATION IN THE MIDDLE EAST

Fashion education is a crucial component of the industry, providing designers and entrepreneurs with the necessary skills and knowledge to succeed in the competitive and ever-changing global fashion landscape. In the Middle East, fashion education has seen significant growth in recent years, with many institutions and programs emerging to meet the demand for skilled professionals in the industry.

However, despite this growth, fashion education in the Middle East still faces several challenges. One of the primary challenges is the lack of qualified educators and trainers in the industry. Many institutions struggle to attract experienced professionals to teach and mentor their students, which can limit the quality and effectiveness of their programs.

Another challenge is the need to balance traditional cultural norms and expectations with the need for innovation and creativity in fashion education. Many institutions face pressure to adhere to cultural and religious standards of modesty and decorum, which can limit the scope and diversity of their curricula.

Despite these challenges, there are several institutions and programs in the Middle East that are making significant strides in fashion education. For example, the Dubai Institute of Design and Innovation (DIDI) offers a multidisciplinary curriculum that combines fashion design with other design disciplines, such as product and graphic design. The Fashion Design and Technology program at Zayed University in the UAE also provides students with a comprehensive education in fashion design, merchandising, and marketing.

In addition to formal education programs, there are also several initiatives and organizations in the Middle East that are providing training and support for aspiring fashion entrepreneurs. The Dubai Fashion Institute, for example, offers courses and workshops in fashion design, marketing, and business management, while the Qatar Fashion and Design Council provides mentorship and funding opportunities for emerging designers.

In conclusion, while the state of fashion education in the Middle East still faces several challenges, there are several institutions and programs that are making significant strides in providing aspiring designers and entrepreneurs with the necessary skills and knowledge to succeed in the industry. As the industry continues to grow and evolve, it is likely that we will see more innovative and effective fashion education programs and initiatives emerge in the region.

CHAPTER 5: THE RISE OF MODEST WEAR IN THE MIDDLE EAST AND BEYOND

Modest wear, which refers to clothing that covers the body and conforms to religious and cultural standards of modesty, has been a long-standing tradition in the Middle East. However, in recent years, modest wear has become a global fashion trend, appealing to consumers who are looking for clothing that is both fashionable and modest.

The rise of modest wear in the Middle East and beyond is driven by several factors. One of the primary factors is the increasing demand for clothing that is both modest and fashionable, particularly among young Muslim consumers. Modest wear also appeals to consumers who are looking for clothing that is more inclusive and respectful of diverse cultural and religious traditions.

The rise of modest wear has also been supported by the emergence of social media and e-commerce, which have made it easier for consumers to access and purchase modest wear clothing from around the world. This has created new opportunities for modest wear designers and entrepreneurs, who are now able to reach a wider audience and grow their businesses beyond their local markets.

In the Middle East, the rise of modest wear has also led to the emergence of new and innovative fashion trends that incorporate traditional Middle Eastern designs and materials into modern and fashionable clothing. Many designers are also exploring gender-neutral designs and promoting greater acceptance of non-binary identities through their work.

The popularity of modest wear is likely to continue growing in the coming years, as consumers increasingly seek out clothing that is both fashionable and respectful of diverse cultural and religious traditions. This trend is also likely to continue driving innovation and creativity in the Middle Eastern fashion industry, providing new opportunities for designers and entrepreneurs to succeed and grow their businesses.

In conclusion, the rise of modest wear in the Middle East and beyond is a reflection of changing consumer preferences and attitudes towards fashion, as well as the growing demand for clothing that is both fashionable and respectful of diverse cultural and religious traditions. This trend is likely to continue driving innovation and growth in the Middle Eastern fashion industry, providing new opportunities for designers and entrepreneurs to succeed and thrive.

CHAPTER 6: SUSTAINABLE FASHION PRACTICES IN THE MIDDLE EAST

Sustainability has become a major focus in the global fashion industry in recent years, as consumers and industry stakeholders have become increasingly aware of the environmental and social impact of fashion production and consumption. In the Middle East, sustainable fashion practices are gaining traction, as designers and entrepreneurs are exploring new ways to reduce waste, promote ethical production, and support local communities.

One of the key challenges facing sustainable fashion in the Middle East is the limited availability of sustainable materials and production processes. Many designers and entrepreneurs struggle to find sustainable materials that are both affordable and of high quality, while also facing challenges in finding production partners that prioritize ethical and sustainable practices.

However, despite these challenges, there are several initiatives and organizations in the Middle East that are promoting and supporting sustainable fashion practices. For example, the Dubai Design District (d3) hosts an annual sustainability conference, bringing together industry leaders and experts to discuss the latest trends and innovations in sustainable fashion.

There are also several local and regional brands in the Middle East that are leading the way in sustainable fashion. For example,

Bambah Boutique in Dubai incorporates sustainable practices into its production processes, using natural and eco-friendly materials, and supporting local artisans and communities. Another example is Eco Souk, an online marketplace based in Abu Dhabi that offers a range of sustainable and eco-friendly products, including clothing and accessories.

In addition to these initiatives and brands, many Middle Eastern designers are exploring innovative and sustainable design practices, such as upcycling and using natural and recycled materials. These practices not only reduce waste and promote ethical production, but also create unique and distinctive designs that appeal to consumers who are looking for fashion that is both sustainable and fashionable.

In conclusion, sustainable fashion practices are gaining traction in the Middle East, as designers and entrepreneurs explore new ways to reduce waste, promote ethical production, and support local communities. While there are still challenges to be addressed, such as limited availability of sustainable materials and production processes, there are also several initiatives and organizations that are promoting and supporting sustainable fashion practices in the region. As the industry continues to grow and evolve, it is likely that we will see more innovative and sustainable fashion practices emerging from the Middle East.

CHAPTER 7: FASHION AND SOCIAL MEDIA IN THE MIDDLE EAST

Social media has had a significant impact on the global fashion industry, providing designers and entrepreneurs with a new platform to showcase their work, connect with consumers, and promote their brands. In the Middle East, social media has played a particularly important role in shaping the region's fashion landscape, providing a platform for emerging designers and promoting greater diversity and inclusivity in fashion.

One of the primary benefits of social media for fashion in the Middle East is its ability to reach a wide and diverse audience. Platforms such as Instagram, Twitter, and Facebook allow designers and entrepreneurs to connect with consumers from all over the world, providing a global platform for their work.

Social media has also played a role in promoting greater diversity and inclusivity in the Middle Eastern fashion industry. Many designers and entrepreneurs are using social media to challenge traditional gender norms and promote greater acceptance of non-binary identities. They are also using social media to showcase designs that draw inspiration from the region's cultural heritage, celebrating the diversity and richness of Middle Eastern fashion.

In addition to these benefits, social media has also created new opportunities for Middle Eastern designers and entrepreneurs to grow their businesses and reach new audiences. Platforms such as Instagram and Facebook have become important marketing tools, allowing designers and entrepreneurs to showcase their work and reach new customers, without the need for large marketing budgets or extensive networks.

However, social media also presents several challenges for the Middle Eastern fashion industry, particularly around issues of authenticity and transparency. With the rise of social media influencers and sponsored posts, there is a growing concern about the authenticity of social media content, and the influence that sponsored content can have on consumer behavior.

In conclusion, social media has had a significant impact on the Middle Eastern fashion industry, providing designers and entrepreneurs with a new platform to showcase their work, connect with consumers, and promote their brands. While there are challenges associated with the rise of social media, the benefits of greater diversity, inclusivity, and global reach are likely to continue shaping the region's fashion landscape in the years to come.

CHAPTER 8: LUXURY FASHION IN THE MIDDLE EAST

Luxury fashion is an important segment of the global fashion industry, and the Middle East is a significant market for luxury brands. The region has a growing population of high-net-worth individuals, as well as a strong cultural appreciation for luxury goods and experiences.

One of the primary drivers of luxury fashion in the Middle East is the region's strong economy, particularly in countries such as the United Arab Emirates, Qatar, and Saudi Arabia. These countries have seen significant economic growth in recent years, driven by industries such as oil and gas, finance, and tourism, creating a growing population of affluent consumers with a strong appetite for luxury goods.

Another factor driving luxury fashion in the Middle East is the region's cultural appreciation for luxury and opulence. Luxury brands are seen as symbols of status and prestige, and are often associated with Middle Eastern cultural values such as hospitality, generosity, and generosity.

The Middle East is also home to several luxury fashion events and initiatives, such as the Dubai Fashion Week and the Dubai Mall Fashion Avenue, which provide a platform for luxury brands to showcase their latest collections and connect with affluent consumers from around the world.

Despite the growth of luxury fashion in the Middle East, the industry also faces several challenges. One of the primary challenges is the need to balance cultural expectations and religious norms with the global luxury fashion landscape. Many luxury brands have faced criticism for their use of religious and cultural symbols in their designs, raising questions about cultural appropriation and sensitivity.

Another challenge is the need to adapt to changing consumer preferences and attitudes towards sustainability and ethical production. As consumers become more aware of the environmental and social impact of fashion production and consumption, luxury brands in the Middle East will need to find new ways to promote sustainability and ethical practices in their businesses.

In conclusion, luxury fashion is an important segment of the Middle Eastern fashion industry, driven by a growing population of affluent consumers and a cultural appreciation for luxury and opulence. However, the industry also faces challenges around cultural sensitivity and sustainability, and will need to adapt to changing consumer preferences and attitudes in order to remain relevant and successful in the global fashion landscape.

CHAPTER 9: TRADITIONAL CRAFTS AND FASHION IN THE MIDDLE EAST

The Middle East has a rich history of traditional crafts, including weaving, embroidery, and metalwork, that have been used for centuries to create beautiful and intricate textiles and clothing. Today, many designers and entrepreneurs in the region are exploring new ways to incorporate these traditional crafts into modern and fashionable designs, promoting the region's cultural heritage and supporting local communities.

One of the primary benefits of incorporating traditional crafts into fashion is the unique and distinctive designs that can be created. Many Middle Eastern traditional crafts, such as embroidery and weaving, use intricate and colorful patterns that are both visually stunning and culturally meaningful. By incorporating these patterns and techniques into modern fashion designs, designers are able to create clothing that is both fashionable and culturally rich.

Another benefit of incorporating traditional crafts into fashion is the support it provides for local communities and artisans. Many traditional crafts are practiced by local artisans and communities, who often lack the resources and infrastructure to reach wider markets. By incorporating these crafts into fashion, designers and entrepreneurs are able to provide a market for these artisans, promoting their work and supporting their livelihoods.

Despite these benefits, there are also challenges associated with incorporating traditional crafts into fashion, particularly around issues of authenticity and cultural sensitivity. Designers and entrepreneurs must be careful to respect and honor the cultural and historical significance of these traditional crafts, while also promoting their relevance and value in modern fashion.

In addition to these challenges, there is also a need to balance traditional crafts with modern design aesthetics and consumer preferences. Many designers are exploring new ways to update and modernize traditional crafts, incorporating them into contemporary fashion designs that appeal to a wider audience.

In conclusion, incorporating traditional crafts into fashion is an important trend in the Middle Eastern fashion industry, promoting the region's cultural heritage and supporting local communities and artisans. While there are challenges associated with this trend, such as issues of authenticity and cultural sensitivity, the unique and distinctive designs created by incorporating traditional crafts into fashion are likely to continue driving innovation and creativity in the industry.

CHAPTER 10: THE FUTURE OF FASHION IN THE MIDDLE EAST

The Middle Eastern fashion industry has undergone significant transformation in recent years, driven by changing consumer preferences, technological advancements, and increasing global competition. Looking ahead, the industry is likely to continue evolving and adapting to new trends and challenges, while also remaining true to its cultural heritage and identity.

One of the primary trends that is likely to shape the future of fashion in the Middle East is sustainability. As consumers become more aware of the environmental and social impact of fashion production and consumption, there is a growing demand for sustainable and ethical fashion practices. In response, designers and entrepreneurs in the Middle East are likely to explore new ways to promote sustainability and ethical production, while also remaining competitive in the global fashion market.

Another trend that is likely to shape the future of fashion in the Middle East is the rise of technology and innovation. As new technologies such as 3D printing and artificial intelligence continue to transform the global fashion industry, designers and entrepreneurs in the Middle East are likely to explore new ways to incorporate these technologies into their businesses, creating new opportunities for growth and innovation.

The future of fashion in the Middle East is also likely to be shaped by changing consumer preferences and attitudes towards cultural and religious identity. Many designers and entrepreneurs are exploring new ways to promote diversity and inclusivity in their designs, celebrating the richness and diversity of Middle Eastern cultural heritage.

Finally, the future of fashion in the Middle East is likely to be shaped by the ongoing impact of global events such as the COVID-19 pandemic. The pandemic has had a significant impact on the fashion industry, disrupting supply chains, changing consumer behavior, and forcing businesses to adapt to new and evolving challenges. As the industry continues to recover and adapt to the post-pandemic landscape, designers and entrepreneurs in the Middle East are likely to explore new ways to meet the changing needs and expectations of consumers.

In conclusion, the future of fashion in the Middle East is likely to be shaped by a range of trends and challenges, including sustainability, technology and innovation, cultural identity, and global events. As the industry continues to evolve and adapt, it is likely that we will see new and innovative designs and businesses emerge from the region, driving growth and creativity in the global fashion landscape.

CHAPTER 11: CONCLUSION

The Middle Eastern fashion industry is a vibrant and dynamic sector of the global fashion landscape, driven by a rich cultural heritage, a growing population of affluent consumers, and a diverse range of designers and entrepreneurs. While the industry faces several challenges, such as issues around sustainability, cultural sensitivity, and global competition, it is also a sector that is full of opportunities for growth and innovation.

In recent years, the Middle Eastern fashion industry has undergone significant transformation, with designers and entrepreneurs exploring new ways to incorporate traditional crafts, promote diversity and inclusivity, and adapt to changing consumer preferences and attitudes. As the industry continues to evolve and adapt to new trends and challenges, it is likely that we will see new and innovative designs and businesses emerge from the region, driving growth and creativity in the global fashion landscape.

As consumers become increasingly aware of the environmental and social impact of fashion production and consumption, there is also a growing demand for sustainable and ethical fashion practices. Designers and entrepreneurs in the Middle East are well-positioned to respond to this trend, incorporating sustainable practices into their businesses, promoting ethical production, and supporting local communities and artisans.

Looking ahead, the future of fashion in the Middle East is likely to be shaped by a range of trends and challenges, including sustainability, technology and innovation, cultural identity, and global events. While there are challenges associated with each of these trends, there are also opportunities for growth and innovation, as designers and entrepreneurs explore new ways to meet the changing needs and expectations of consumers.

In conclusion, the Middle Eastern fashion industry is a dynamic and exciting sector of the global fashion landscape, full of opportunities for growth and innovation. As the industry continues to evolve and adapt to new trends and challenges, it is likely that we will see new and innovative designs and businesses emerge from the region, driving growth and creativity in the global fashion landscape.

FINAL THOUGHTS

The Middle Eastern fashion industry is a sector that is full of energy, creativity, and innovation. From traditional crafts and textiles to modern and innovative designs, the industry reflects the region's unique identity and cultural heritage, while also exploring new ways to incorporate sustainability, technology, and cultural identity into its businesses.

As the industry continues to evolve and adapt to new trends and challenges, it is important to recognize the contributions of all stakeholders in shaping the region's fashion landscape. From designers and entrepreneurs to artisans and consumers, each plays a vital role in creating a fashion industry that is dynamic, socially responsible, and aesthetically compelling.

At the same time, there are challenges that the industry faces, particularly around issues of sustainability, cultural sensitivity, and global competition. By working together to address these challenges, stakeholders in the industry can help to create a more inclusive and sustainable fashion industry that reflects the richness and diversity of the Middle East.

In conclusion, the Middle Eastern fashion industry is a sector that is full of potential and promise, driven by a deep cultural heritage and a passion for innovation and creativity. As the industry continues to grow and evolve, it is likely that we will see new and exciting designs and businesses emerge from the region, shaping the global fashion landscape in new and exciting ways.

Acknowledgements

The writing of this book would not have been possible without the contributions of a wide range of individuals and organizations. We would like to express our gratitude to all those who have helped to shape the Middle Eastern fashion industry, including designers, entrepreneurs, artisans, and consumers.

We would also like to acknowledge the support of organizations such as the Dubai Design and Fashion Council, which has been instrumental in promoting the region's fashion industry and supporting emerging designers and entrepreneurs.

Finally, we would like to thank our readers for their interest and engagement with the Middle Eastern fashion industry. We hope that this book has provided a comprehensive and informative overview of the industry, highlighting its strengths and challenges, and inspiring readers to explore the richness and diversity of the region's fashion landscape.

We look forward to the continued growth and success of the Middle Eastern fashion industry, and to the contributions of all those who are working to shape its future.

EPILOGUE

The Middle Eastern fashion industry has a long and rich history, spanning centuries of cultural heritage, craftsmanship, and innovation. Today, the industry is at the forefront of the global fashion landscape, showcasing a diverse range of designs, styles, and trends that reflect the region's unique identity and cultural heritage.

As the industry continues to evolve and adapt to new trends and challenges, it is important to recognize the contributions of designers, entrepreneurs, artisans, and consumers in shaping the region's fashion landscape. From traditional crafts and textiles to modern and innovative designs, the Middle Eastern fashion industry continues to inspire and captivate audiences around the world.

Looking ahead, the future of fashion in the Middle East is bright, with new opportunities for growth, innovation, and creativity. As designers and entrepreneurs explore new ways to incorporate sustainability, technology, and cultural identity into their businesses, they are helping to shape a fashion industry that is both dynamic and socially responsible.

At the same time, it is important to acknowledge the challenges that the industry faces, particularly around issues of sustainability, cultural sensitivity, and global competition. By working together to address these challenges, designers, entrepreneurs, and consumers can help to create a more inclusive and sustainable fashion industry that reflects the richness and diversity of the Middle East.

In conclusion, the Middle Eastern fashion industry is a unique and vibrant sector of the global fashion landscape, driven by a rich cultural heritage and a diverse range of designers, entrepreneurs, and artisans. As the industry continues to evolve and adapt to new trends and challenges, it is likely that we will see new and innovative designs and businesses emerge from the region, helping to shape a fashion industry that is both socially responsible and aesthetically compelling.

APPENDIX

In this appendix, we provide a glossary of terms related to the Middle Eastern fashion industry, as well as a list of key designers and entrepreneurs in the region.

ABOUT THE AUTHOR

Manju Batth

Manju Batth (Full name Manjit Kaur Batth) is a talented fashion designer who was born in India and raised in Germany. Her passion for fashion has taken her around the globe, and she draws inspiration from different cultures to create truly unique and exclusive dresses.

Manju's love for fashion began at a young age, and she spent countless hours sketching and designing her own clothes. Her parents encouraged her to pursue her passion, and she went on to study fashion design in Germany, Austria, and Italy. She worked for several fashion houses and gained valuable experience in the industry.

One of Manju's defining characteristics as a designer is her admiration for fashion worldwide. She travels extensively and uses her experiences to inform her designs. Her dresses are not just beautiful pieces of luxury clothing, but they are also a reflection of the cultures and impressions she has encountered on her travels.

What sets Manju apart from other designers is her commitment to exclusivity. She only creates one dress per design and does not engage in mass production. She believes that every individual is unique and deserves to feel special. By making only one dress, she ensures that her clients are getting a truly exclusive piece that nobody else in the world will have.

Manju's dresses are truly exceptional. She uses the finest materials and pays attention to every detail to create dresses that are both stunning and comfortable to wear. Her designs are suitable for a wide range of occasions, from red carpet events to weddings, and each one is tailor-made to the client's specific needs.

In conclusion, Manju Batth is a fashion designer who has made a name for herself by creating exclusive and unique dresses inspired by cultures around the world. Her commitment to individuality and attention to detail make her designs truly exceptional, and her clients are guaranteed to receive a one-of-a-kind dress that will make them feel special and beautiful.

RECOMMENDATIONS

For readers who are interested in learning more about the Middle Eastern fashion industry, there are several resources that may be of interest. These include:

Fashion Weeks: The Middle East is home to several prominent fashion weeks, including Dubai Fashion Week, Arab Fashion Week, and Saudi Arabian Fashion Week. These events provide a platform for emerging and established designers to showcase their latest collections and connect with industry professionals.

Fashion Museums: Several museums in the Middle East are dedicated to showcasing the region's fashion heritage, including the Museum of Islamic Art in Qatar and the Bahrain National Museum. These museums provide a unique opportunity to learn about the history and evolution of fashion in the region.

Online Communities: There are several online communities and forums dedicated to discussing fashion in the Middle East, including Middle East Fashion and Fashion Forward Dubai. These communities provide a platform for designers, entrepreneurs, and consumers to connect and exchange ideas.

Fashion Publications: There are several fashion publications that cover the Middle Eastern fashion industry, including Harper's Bazaar Arabia, Vogue Arabia, and Grazia Middle East. These publications provide insights into the latest trends, styles, and designers in the region.

Design and Fashion Schools: Several design and fashion schools in the Middle East, including the American University in Dubai and the Dubai Institute of Design and Innovation, offer courses and programs in fashion design and entrepreneurship. These schools provide a valuable resource for aspiring designers and entrepreneurs looking to develop their skills and knowledge in the industry.

In conclusion, there are several resources available for readers who are interested in learning more about the Middle Eastern fashion industry. By exploring these resources and engaging with the industry, readers can gain a deeper appreciation for the region's rich cultural heritage and unique contributions to the global fashion landscape.

GLOSSARY OF TERMS:

Abaya: A traditional, loose-fitting cloak worn by women in the Middle East.

Kaftan: A traditional, loose-fitting garment worn by both men and women in the Middle East.

Hijab: A headscarf worn by Muslim women as a sign of modesty and religious observance.

Thobe: A traditional, ankle-length garment worn by men in the Middle East.

Keffiyeh: A traditional headscarf worn by men in the Middle East, typically made of cotton or wool.

Jellabiya: A traditional, loose-fitting garment worn by men and women in the Middle East.

KEY DESIGNERS AND ENTREPRENEURS:

Elie Saab: A Lebanese fashion designer known for his luxurious and elegant designs.

Reem Acra: A Lebanese fashion designer known for her bridal wear and red carpet gowns.

Zuhair Murad: A Lebanese fashion designer known for his intricate and ornate designs.

Mary Katrantzou: A Greek fashion designer based in London, known for her vibrant and colorful prints.

Razan Alazzouni: A Saudi Arabian fashion designer known for her modern and sophisticated designs.

Madiyah Al Sharqi: An Emirati fashion designer known for her feminine and elegant designs.

Hussein Bazaza: A Lebanese fashion designer known for his innovative and experimental designs.

Aiisha Ramadan: A Lebanese fashion designer known for her feminine and contemporary designs.

Bambah Boutique: An Emirati fashion brand known for its vintage-inspired designs.

Bouguessa: An Emirati fashion brand known for its modest and elegant designs.

In conclusion, this glossary and list of key designers and entrepreneurs provides a snapshot of the diversity and creativity of the Middle Eastern fashion industry. By exploring these terms and individuals, readers can gain a deeper understanding of the region's unique contributions to the global fashion landscape.

FURTHER READING

For readers who are interested in exploring the Middle Eastern fashion industry in greater depth, there are several books and articles that may be of interest. These include:

"The Politics of Fashion in the Middle East" by Andrew M. Robinson and Annemarie Strassel: This book explores the intersection of fashion, politics, and culture in the Middle East, providing insights into the ways in which fashion is used to express identity, challenge social norms, and shape public discourse.

"Fashion in the Middle East" by M. Angela Jansen: This book provides a comprehensive overview of the history and evolution of fashion in the Middle East, from traditional garments and textiles to modern and innovative designs.

"Fashion in the Middle East: Trends and Developments" by Faiza Bouguessa: This article provides insights into the latest trends and developments in the Middle Eastern fashion industry, exploring the ways in which designers and entrepreneurs are responding to changing consumer preferences and attitudes.

"The State of the Middle Eastern Fashion Industry" by Hafsa Lodi: This article provides a comprehensive overview of the current state of the Middle Eastern fashion industry, exploring the challenges and opportunities facing designers, entrepreneurs, and consumers in the region.

"Crafting Modernity: The Reinvention of Middle Eastern Fashion" by Maysa Dabbagh: This article explores the ways in which designers in the Middle East are reinterpreting traditional crafts and textiles in order to create modern and innovative designs that reflect the

region's unique cultural heritage.

In conclusion, these resources provide valuable insights into the history, evolution, and current state of the Middle Eastern fashion industry. By exploring these works, readers can gain a deeper appreciation for the region's unique contributions to the global fashion landscape, as well as the challenges and opportunities facing the industry as it continues to grow and evolve.

www.ingramcontent.com/pod-product-compliance
Lightning Source LLC
Chambersburg PA
CBHW050752250726
48662CB00005B/2171